Discovering *ART*

Animation

Stuart A. Kallen

ReferencePoint
Press®

San Diego, CA

About the Author

Stuart A. Kallen is the author of more than 250 nonfiction books for children and young adults. He has written on topics ranging from the theory of relativity to the history of rock and roll. In addition, Kallen has written award-winning children's videos and television scripts. In his spare time he is a singer/songwriter/guitarist in San Diego.

© 2015 ReferencePoint Press, Inc.
Printed in the United States

For more information, contact:
ReferencePoint Press, Inc.
PO Box 27779
San Diego, CA 92198
www.ReferencePointPress.com

LIBRARY OF CONGRESS CATALOGING-IN-PUBLICATION DATA

Kallen, Stuart A., 1955–
  Animation / by Stuart A. Kallen.
    pages cm -- (Discovering art)
  ISBN-13: 978-1-60152-664-9 (hardback)
  ISBN-10: 1-60152-664-4 (hardback)
  1. Animated films—Juvenile literature. I. Title.
NC1765.K35 2014
791.43'34--dc23
                                        2013047008

Contents

What Is the Art of Animation?

Animation professor Vibeke Sorensen writes, "Animation is the art of motion, and art in motion."[1] Animators use pens, ink, paint, clay, computers, and other tools to create artistic characters that exaggerate reality in every possible way. Animals talk and make jokes, people travel through time or visit distant planets, and characters walk away from falls, explosions, car crashes, and otherwise deadly incidents. When done successfully, audiences tend to overlook such absurd situations and accept characters as believable personalities with human emotions.

The world's most famous cartoon producer, Walt Disney, owed his success to the authentic characters he created. As animation expert John Canemaker writes, Disney believed moviegoers "would so deeply relate to the characters' personalities that they would laugh *with* them (not *at* them), fear for their safety, and weep at their demise. Such a major suspension of disbelief required storytelling and animation skills (or magic) never seen before."[2]

Brilliant animation skills are only the first step in the long, complex process of creating animated films. Since the late 1930s, when Disney began making full-length animated features such

> **Words in Context**
> *suspension of disbelief*
> The willingness of a viewer or reader to overlook implausible situations in a film or book and accept the premise of a story—even if it involves talking animals.

as *Snow White and the Seven Dwarfs*, animated characters were enlisted to tell complex, believable stories with many twists and turns. The tales played out in front of magnificent scenes and backdrops with colors more vivid than those found in real life.

Art in Motion

Animators are artists, and many have studied animal and human anatomy. In the 1930s and 1940s, Disney required his animators to watch live-action films of acrobats, dancers, wrestlers, and even reptiles and barnyard animals. One of those animators, Hamilton Luske, was famous for closely observing movements of various objects even in social situations. Luske would comment on the way his tie fluttered in the wind while he was on a sailboat or the way his friend's body twisted when hitting a golf ball. These motions

Walt Disney's *Snow White and the Seven Dwarfs*, released in 1937, sought to create a graceful and believable animated female character in Snow White. Disney also gave each of the dwarfs a memorable and recognizable personality.

informed character movements in Disney animated films such as *Cinderella* and *Peter Pan*. In describing Luske's work on the Disney cartoon *Pinocchio* (1940), animator Tom Sito explained, "The gestures and the acting are so perfect that the characters cease to exist as drawings, you accept them as living individuals."[3]

A New Reality

Popular animation relies on great characters acting out a compelling story, but putting art into motion is a long and complex technical process. It involves teams of animators, voice actors, scriptwriters, video technicians, sound editors, and numerous other filmmaking wizards.

Since its beginnings in the early 1900s, animation has been a fascinating combination of artistic skill, complex filmmaking techniques, and show business. The public loves animation because characters can tell stories and visit worlds as infinite as the imagination. As film and media critic Marián Steiner explains, "Constructing a new reality frame-by-frame brought artists endless possibilities for entertainment, artistic expression, and for playing various tricks with the viewer's eyes and mind, without the limitations and constraints of reality."[4]

Chapter One

Early Animation

At the beginning of the twentieth century, before the advent of radio, television, and movies, Americans received most of their news and entertainment from newspapers. There were about twenty thousand daily, weekly, and monthly newspapers printed across the country, and cities like New York, Chicago, and San Francisco had numerous competing dailies. Most carried popular comic strips, or funnies, like the *Katzenjammer Kids*, *Mutt and Jeff*, and *Hogan's Alley*.

While the comics masqueraded as entertainment for children, they were also loved by adult readers. The black and-white daily funnies featured a cast of crazy characters who also appeared on Sundays in full-color on full-page spreads.

Little Nemo in Slumberland

In the early days of animation, several characters from the funny pages were reborn as animated cartoons. And some of the earliest animators also worked as comic strip artists.

One of the most popular comic strips of the era, *Little Nemo in Slumberland*, first appeared in 1905. Created by the artist Windsor McCay, *Little Nemo* followed the antics of a seven-year-old boy who traveled through Slumberland, an outlandish dream world consisting of weird fantasies, strange phantoms, and wild reveries. Literary critic Stefan Kanfer explains:

> Nothing in Nemo's universe was stable. Time and mass became meaningless. Familiar objects could be cooperative or treasonous. Animals that never walked upon the earth—a

blue camel, a green dragon, a hundred-foot-high turkey—went galumphing over the ground or hurtling through a celestial backdrop. The ground could open up and swallow the walker, and free fall, one of humanity's elemental terrors, was a constant occurrence.[5]

McCay made every Sunday comic a work of art with delicate colors and illustrations modeled on the art nouveau, or new art, style popularized in France in the late nineteenth century. This highly decorative style was characterized by gracefully flowing curved lines and ornamental flower and plant patterns.

McCay incorporated his undulating art nouveau lines in illustrations of horse-size rabbits pulling carriages, airships traveling to Mars, buildings growing on plantlike stalks from the city sidewalk, and starbursts of fireworks streaking across the sky. The lines gave the drawings a sense of motion, and sometimes Little Nemo would crash through the margin of one panel into the next. As John Canemaker explains, "*Little Nemo in Slumberland* was unlike any comic strip before or since. . . . [It] represented a major creative leap, far grander in scope, imagination, color, design, and motion experimentation than any previous . . . comic strip."[6]

McCay's Cartoon Movies

In 1909 McCay began searching for ways to bring his imaginative artwork alive through animation. He found inspiration in the flip books his son traded with friends. The flip book uses a series of drawings or photographs, each slightly different than the next. When a person uses his or her thumb to quickly fan through the pages, the images appear to move, suggesting a fluid sequence of events such as a boy bouncing a ball or a girl walking a dog. This early form of animation inspired McCay, who stated, "From this germ I evolved the modern cartoon movies."[7]

At the time, the motion picture business was in its infancy but growing rapidly. America's first movie theater opened in Pittsburgh in 1905, and by 1909 there were about four thousand movie theaters in the United States. At this time films were only a few minutes long and were silent; though they featured live actors, the actors had no spoken lines. When words were necessary to advance the plot, a title card appeared on the screen.

Silent movies were shot at sixteen frames per second; each second of film was composed of sixteen still pictures that represented motion on a screen when run through a projector. To create animation for *Little Nemo*, McCay needed to make 16 drawings for every second of film—or 960 drawings for each minute of animation. McCay made each drawing with india ink on sheets of translucent rice paper. When he finished the first sketch, he laid a second sheet on top of the original and redrew the characters' arms, legs, hands, feet, mouth, and eyes in a slightly different position. More pictures were painstakingly drawn and layered—one on top of another. When the hundreds of drawings were transferred to film and projected onto a screen, McCay's characters appeared to walk, jump, speak, blink their eyes, and make other movements.

> **Words in Context**
> *frame*
> In the silent film era, each second of film was composed of sixteen still images, each referred to as a frame. In later years movies contained twenty-four or thirty frames per second of film.

Little Nemo in Slumberland mixed about six minutes of live action with four minutes of animation. The live scenes are comical, showing McCay at work surrounded by towering piles of drawing paper and large wooden barrels labeled "ink." The animated scenes feature familiar characters from the comic strip, including Flip, Impy, Little Nemo, and the Princess. The first seconds show the green clown Flip with a cigar in his mouth. The words "Watch me move" appear over Flip's head. Canemaker describes the animated sequence:

> There are no backgrounds, just limitless limbo. Perspective is indicated by the enlargement and reduction of figure sizes. There is no plot and the characters appear magically as abstract lines that metamorphose into Impy, Nemo, and the Princess. There is continual movement in the film; Nemo is formed by lines resembling steel filings attracted to a magnet (he is resplendent in a red cape and hat with red and yellow plumes);

Impy and Flip contort their forms as if they were fun house mirrors; Nemo sketches the form of the Princess, she comes to life, and a rose grows just in time to be picked for her by Nemo. As a grand finale, a magnificent three-dimensionally drawn and animated green dragon–chariot carries off the two children to Slumberland.[8]

Animated Personality

When *Little Nemo* was shown in theaters, people did not know what to make of the smooth, natural movements of the meticulously hand-drawn characters; no one had ever seen animation before. Audiences assumed McCay was stringing together a series of photos much like those seen in flip books. This frustrated McCay, who stated, "My audiences declared that it was not a drawing but that the pictures were photographs of real children."[9]

To prove his drawings were not trick photography, McCay created his next cartoon in 1914 with an extinct creature performing deeds that could not be mistaken for reality. *Gertie the Dinosaur* shows a lovable dinosaur lumbering across the landscape, eating a tree, drinking an entire lake, and performing tricks like a circus elephant.

McCay created a total of ten highly successful animated films, including *The Story of a Mosquito* and *Bug Vaudeville*. Canemaker describes McCay's groundbreaking work: "The fluid motion, the naturalistic timing, feeling of weight, and . . . the attempts to inject individualistic personality traits into his characters are qualities that McCay first brought to the animated film medium."[10]

Words in Context

short
Any film that is forty minutes or less, as opposed to feature films, which are usually around ninety minutes or more.

Simplifying the Animation Process

Audiences loved the silly antics of McCay's animated dinosaurs and bugs, but producing these films was less than profitable. The twelve-minute *Gertie the Dinosaur* took McCay about eight months to produce, and his labor intensive process significantly cut into any po-

Windsor McCay created *Gertie the Dinosaur* (1914) to show audiences who had never before seen animation that his animated films did not consist of photographs. McCay's twelve-minute, black and white, meticulously hand-drawn animated film took about eight months to complete.

tential profits. With audiences demanding a regular supply of brief animated films, called shorts, cartoonist John R. Bray recognized an opportunity. Although he appreciated McCay's exacting, hand-drawn work, Bray wished to make money as quickly as possible. This led him to state, "I wanted to simplify the process so that cartoons could be supplied as a regular feature—as many as the public wanted."[11] To that end, Bray began using the cel animation process in 1914.

Cels are transparent plastic sheets made of cellulose acetate or cellulose nitrate, the same material used to make movie film. Cels are either 10 by 12 inches (25.4 by 30.5 cm) or 14 by 16 inches (35.6 by 40.6 cm). The cel animation process had advantages over McCay's methods. The animator no longer had to redraw the character and backgrounds on each sheet. As cartoon historian Charles Solomon explains:

The transparent cels made . . . printed backgrounds unnecessary. The characters could be drawn on cels and laid over a single background, or vice versa. If only part of the character was moving, that part could be drawn on one cel level and laid over a drawing of the rest of the character. If [a character] was raising his arm, his head and body would be on one cel; a series of cels with the arm in successive positions would be placed on top, one at a time.[12]

Colonel Heeza Liar

The use of cells saved huge amounts of time and money, which helped them become the industry standard. Spotting an opportunity, Bray began mass-producing animated films. His studio, Bray Productions, operated an assembly line staffed by nine former newspaper cartoonists, four camera operators, and thirty art assistants. In 1915 Bray signed a deal with Paramount Pictures to produce one complete cartoon each week—considered an astounding accomplishment for the time. Each film lasted nine to ten minutes and required the creation of up to ten thousand cels. Because each cartoon took about a month to produce, Bray set up four units that worked overlapping schedules to keep up the steady flow of work.

Bray's animators drew rough pencil sketches of a cartoon on paper and then copied character outlines onto cels using ink. An assistant then filled in solid black areas, erased small errors, and painted backgrounds.

As a former cartoonist, Bray worked alongside his animators. A publicity sheet from Bray's studio describes how he perfected the art of animating animals: "For months he haunted the Bronx Zoo in order to study the animals there and analyze their motions. He even bought a large farm across the Hudson [River] from Poughkeepsie and stocked it with various animals in order to further extend his knowledge of animal anatomy."[13]

Bray's most famous creation was the pot-bellied Colonel Heeza Liar, the first recurring cartoon character in animation history. Liar moved from the funny pages to the movie screen in 1913 and appeared in fifty-eight animated films before he was retired in 1924. During this time the colonel spun tall tales about being shipwrecked, playing baseball, traveling as a hobo, and even fighting in World War I. The

Bringing *Little Nemo* to the Screen

When Windsor McCay created the first animated cartoon, *Little Nemo*, he had to invent techniques to make the animated sequence appear smooth and lifelike when filmed. To do so, he drew four thousand drawings on translucent rice paper mounted on cardboard about 9 inches (23 cm) square. The corners of each drawing had registration marks—crosses placed precisely in the same location on the left and right upper corners of each sheet. Registration marks allowed McCay to keep each drawing in alignment with the previous illustration and the one that followed. In addition, the drawings were individually numbered so they could be filmed in the proper order.

When finished, each drawing was set in a sturdy wooden mount, called an animation stand. This was placed in front of a movie camera that used black-and-white 16 mm film (film that was 16 millimeters, or 0.63 inches wide). The animation camera was customized to shoot one frame of film at a time. After one drawing was shot, it was removed and the next one was placed in the animation stand. In this way, sixteen drawings made up 1 second of film and McCay's four thousand drawings created about 250 seconds, or 4 minutes and 10 seconds, of animation.

antics of Liar were familiar to everyone who went to a movie theater because cartoons were always shown before movies during the 1920s. In addition to Colonel Heeza Liar, Bray Productions created other recurring characters, including Farmer Al Falfa, Bobby Bumps, and a duck husband and wife named Danny Daddles and Quacky Doodles.

"Hyper-Realistic Animation"

Bray Productions created more than 545 animated films between 1913 and 1927. Among the dozens of artists attracted to the studio was Max Fleischer, a cartoonist with the *Brooklyn Daily Eagle*.

Fleischer had noticed a problem with Bray's cartoons. Because the animated sequences were produced quickly, the movements of the characters were often repetitive and the ink lines jittery. Fleischer wanted to bring more fluid lines and more realism to Bray's animated characters. To do so, around 1915, Fleischer invented a machine called a rotoscope. This invention made it possible to use live-action film footage to create cartoon cels.

Rotoscoping began with a live actor who was filmed dancing, jumping, tumbling, and performing other cartoonish moves in front of a bare white backdrop. The finished movie was fed into a rotoscope, which consisted of a specialized movie camera set up to advance the film one frame at a time. The camera projected each frame of the mov-

A series of hand-drawn images, or storyboard, shows the consecutive movements of a dancer. When projected on a rotoscope, the movements seemed smooth and lifelike. The rotoscope also helped to eliminate jittering on the screen, a common problem in early animated films.

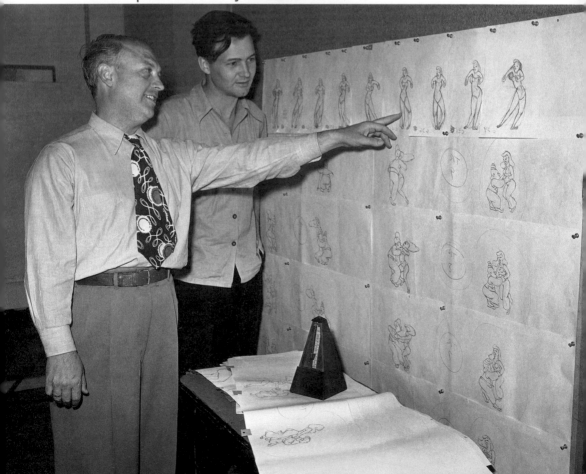

ie on a piece of frosted glass mounted on an artist easel. An animator stood in front of the easel and used a pen and ink to trace the images on each frame onto a cel. This captured every movement, gesture, and expression of the live actor in the film. As animation historian Noell K. Wolfgram Evans describes it, "The rotoscope process was used to create hyper-realistic animation with the result looking as if a traditional live-action film and an animated short had a child."[14]

Fleischer spent several years perfecting the rotoscoping technique with the help of his brother Dave. In 1919 the Fleischer brothers used rotoscoping to produce their first commercial animation series. The *Out of the Inkwell* cartoons featured Ko-Ko the Clown and his white dog, Fritz. Like *Little Nemo*, episodes of *Out of the Inkwell* mixed live and animated action. Most *Inkwell* cartoons began with an appearance by Max Fleischer, who either started to draw various parts of the clown or blew on an ink blob to bring Ko-Ko to life. In one cartoon a half-finished Ko-Ko grabs a pen from the animator and finishes drawing himself.

The *Out of the Inkwell* stories were very clever, and the mischievous Ko-Ko often mocked authorities and broke society's rules. This made the cartoon a huge hit with audiences. Critics raved about Ko-Ko's smooth, supple motions when he walked, danced, and leaped like a graceful athlete. In 1920 a *New York Times* critic compared the high-quality *Out of the Inkwell* with other, less artistic cartoons of the time: "Ko-Ko does not jerk himself from one position to another, nor does he move an arm and a leg while the remainder of his body remains as unnaturally still—as if it were fixed in ink lines on paper."[15]

The World-Famous Felix

Out of the Inkwell was one of the major animated series of the silent era and spawned a host of imitators. A little boy named Dinky Doodle and his dog Pete the Pup were created by cartoonist Walter

Felix the Cat rose to popularity in the 1920s—and remains popular today. Felix's creator, Otto Messmer, used all different eye motions to give his character appealing facial expressions.

Lantz, who often appeared on-screen with his characters. Perhaps the most enduring character of the era was Felix the Cat, created by Otto Messmer.

Felix the Cat, who lives on today in countless cartoons, toys, stuffed animals, and even parodies, began by chance in 1919. Messmer worked for Pat Sullivan, whose company created cartoons for Paramount Pictures. Messmer picks up the story:

> Sullivan's studio was very busy, and Paramount, they were falling behind their schedule and they needed one extra [cartoon] to fill in. And Sullivan, being very busy, said, "If you want to do it on the side, you can do any little thing to satisfy them." So I figured a cat would be about the simplest. Make him all

black, you know—you wouldn't need to worry about outlines. And one gag after the other, you know? Cute. And they all got laughs. So Paramount liked it so they ordered a series.[16]

By 1925 Felix the Cat was a huge hit. According to Solomon, "It has been estimated that three-quarters of the world's population had seen or could recognize Felix at the height of his fame."[17] By 1928 the

Animating *Mutt and Jeff*

Dick Huemer began working as an animator in 1916 and went on to become one of the top animation directors for Walt Disney in the 1930s. Huemer was eighty-two years old in 1980 when he described the animation process of the silent era to an interviewer. He explained how he made twenty or more drawings per hour when he made the *Mutt and Jeff* cartoons. Huemer recalled:

> In those days we did a lot of hold positions and just moved maybe an eye. When a character talked, all we'd have was a repeat and reverse of a mouth movement and the rest of the figure didn't move at all. . . . And then the mouth, just this little bit, was on paper. Then a [speech] balloon would come out, with lettering, and hold and then explode. As [Mutt's] mouth manipulated, the balloon came up very quickly, just the bloop!, in about five drawings, and held while you read the balloon. And then it whirled away or exploded. We had various ways of accomplishing that. Characters did violent takes, like all the hair flying off. Once I had all the features flying off in the air, whirl around, and come back and slap on Mutt's face.

Quoted in Danny Peary and Gerald Peary, eds, *The American Animated Cartoon*. New York: Dutton, 1980, p. 34.

little black cat had appeared in more than 165 cartoons and was featured in a successful line of merchandise, including clocks, ceramics, postcards, and stuffed animals.

Like Little Nemo and Ko-Ko, Felix delighted both children and adults. Messmer explains Felix's appeal: "I had him sparkling all the time. Most of the [characters in other] cartoons were like a dummy, just jumping—so I used an extreme amount of eye motion, wriggling the eyes and turning his whiskers, and this seemed to be what hit the public—expressions!"[18]

The Work Lives On

During the era of silent films, animators brought memorable characters to the screen through the use of sparkling expressions, unique personality traits, and fantastic artwork. While some—like Messmer, McCay, and the Fleischers—are remembered by animation fans, hundreds more worked in obscurity as assistant artists, inkers, and camera operators.

By relying on talent, hard work, and persistent dedication to the arts, the animators produced thousands of silent cartoons before sound was introduced to movies in 1928. While the animators of the silent era are gone, their works live on. Felix, Little Nemo, Heeza Liar, Ko-Ko and countless others found new life on the Internet in the twenty-first century, and their escapades can be seen on dozens of video-sharing websites. While the characters remain silent, they continue to communicate through animated actions; cartoons from another century with a timeless quality that continues to amuse in the modern world.

Chapter Two

Animation's Golden Age

On November 18, 1928, audiences saw—and heard—something different at the Colony Theatre in New York City. When the animated short *Steamboat Willie* premiered, it featured a new character, Mickey Mouse. Unlike the sinister-looking rodents often seen in earlier cartoons, Mickey was tall and cheerful. Created by Walt Disney and animator Ub Iwerks, Mickey Mouse stood on two legs and had an upturned face with a wide, friendly grin and big eyes. In *Steamboat Willie* Mickey hopped along with the lively, traditional tunes "Steamboat Bill" and "Turkey in the Straw." Audiences not only saw Mickey dance in perfect time to the music, they heard him beating on pots, pans, garbage cans, and a washboard. He even played xylophone music on the teeth of a cow.

Steamboat Willie was the first animated film produced with synchronized sound, or sound that perfectly meshes with the mouths and body movements of the characters. Disney was inspired to add sound to *Steamboat Willie* after viewing the first movie ever made with synchronized sound, *The Jazz Singer* (1927). Disney told his brother and business partner, Roy Disney, that the new sound technology was an "extreme novelty"[19] that could be used to distinguish Mickey Mouse from all other cartoon characters.

Producing *Steamboat Willie* with synchronized sound proved to be a good business decision. Audiences liked it so much they often cheered, whistled, and applauded when the cartoon ended.

The Visualized Possibilities of the Storyboard

One of Disney's advancements occurred in the studio's story department. On any given day, hundreds of character and scene drawings were spread out haphazardly on tables, desks, and floors. Within this chaotic environment, lead animators worked with scriptwriters and joke writers to create new cartoons. To bring order to this chaos, Disney created what he called storyboards. These consisted of corkboards on walls, where the drawings, which looked like those in comic books, could be pinned in chronological order. Storyboards were first used in the creation of the 1933 cartoon *Three Little Pigs*.

With storyboards, animation directors could move, add, remove, or change sketches to alter the look or chronology of the cartoon. This allowed directors to plot the story, pacing, and rhythm of a cartoon before production. As Disney explained in a 1934 memo to animators, the storyboard was "an ideal way to present your stories because it then shows the visualized possibilities, rather than a lot of words."[22]

Inkers and Inbetweeners

The first step in the new assembly-line animation process involved artists known as "inbetweeners." These animators used ink to draw the numerous cels required to depict smooth movements between major positions, or key poses. After the cels left the in-between department, they went through the next step in the process. Cleanup artists made sure the lines were constant from frame to frame. This prevented characters from appearing to wiggle and jump around onscreen.

In 1932 Disney began producing full-color animations with an expensive film process called Technicolor. When cartoons were shot in Technicolor, they underwent a final step. The inked cels were sent

Synchronized Sound for
Steamboat Willie

When Walt Disney decided to add sound to his cartoons, it required a new level of planning for the animators; the movements of the characters had to be precisely coordinated with the music. Disney's first Mickey Mouse cartoon, the 1928 *Steamboat Willie*, featured numerous sound effects, including Mickey tooting a boat whistle and beating on pots and pans with spoons. There were also many animal noises, including a goat bleating, a cow mooing, a parrot squawking, and chickens cackling.

For *Steamboat Willie*, animator Ub Iwerks illustrated each scene in a series of polished sketches joined with a typed summary of the scene. Disney animator Wilfred Jackson, who had some knowledge of music, created what was called a bar sheet—a chart that paired each measure of music with each scene. Using the bar sheets, Walt Disney prepared exposure sheets, or ex-sheets. These contained frame-by-frame instructions for the camera operators, which explained where musical beats would fall in the frames. With ex-sheets and bar sheets, Disney had unparalleled control over the timing of the animation. After a silent *Steamboat Willie* was completed, a live orchestra recorded the soundtrack while the film played. Sound effects were added later.

When *Steamboat Willie* premiered at the Colony Theatre in New York City on November 18, 1928, it was an instant hit. Viewers might not have understood the technical details of synchronized sound, but they loved Mickey Mouse and his girlfriend Minnie, who also appeared in the cartoon.

to the paint department, where they were colored with paints specially formulated to adhere to the plastic cel material.

While characters were inked and painted, backgrounds of scenes were painted by special background artists. Because the backgrounds are seen on-screen for longer periods of time, they were created with great attention to detail, shading, and perspective.

After the artwork was finished, cels were filmed in a manner developed during the silent era. Each cel was laid on top of a background drawing mounted on a horizontal surface. A heavy sheet of glass, called a platen, was laid over each cel to hold it in place. A movie camera pointed down at the artwork, and one frame of film was shot of each cel.

The Development of Character Types

Disney's techniques resulted in cartoon stars with personality traits that audiences could instantly understand through body language, facial features, and other characteristics. For example, silly characters like Goofy had long, skinny necks, small heads held forward, droopy eyes, no chin, buck teeth, long arms, enormous feet, and protruding stomachs. A tough bad-guy character like the Big Bad Wolf in *Three Little Pigs* was drawn with a small head, barrel chest, no neck, heavy eyebrows, close-set eyes, large chin and jowls, small hips, and short, heavy legs. Cute characters like Mickey Mouse were drawn with the basic proportions of a human baby. They had small ears, elongated pear-shaped bodies, large heads, fat legs, small feet, and high foreheads with wide-spaced eyes low on the head. A screwball character like Donald Duck featured an elongated head, pear-shaped body, low forehead, big feet, and exaggerated facial features such as huge eyes.

Disney was not the only animation studio during this era, and variations of the standard character types were used at other studios. Animators Friz Freleng, Tex Avery, and Bob Clampett, who all worked for Warner Brothers Pictures, used screwball features on Bugs Bunny, the cute baby look on Tweety Bird, and the bully traits for Yosemite Sam. During the golden age of animation, the Warner Brothers animated series *Looney Tunes* and *Merrie Melodies* produced numerous other iconic characters, including Porky Pig, Elmer Fudd, Daffy Duck, Wile E. Coyote, and the Road Runner.

Warner animators created unique cartoons that featured implausible and ridiculous slapstick comedy. Anvils dropped on characters' heads and shotguns blew up in their faces. As animation journalist Michael Crandol notes:

> Tex Avery and Bob Clampett broke from the Disney tradition that the other studios had begun to mimic and imbibed their films with highly exaggerated slapstick comedy. In Avery's "Porky's Duck Hunt" (the first appearance of Daffy Duck, 1937) and Clampett's "Porky in Wackyland" (1938), the characters appear at first to be of the naturalist Disney school, but are constantly distorted beyond all rationality, defying every law of physics for comedic effect. The other Warner artists immediately picked up on the style, and eventually every other studio . . . adopted the method. Slapstick ultimately proved to be the theatrical genre animation was best suited for.[23]

Incorporating Acting Principles

While Warner Brothers animators focused on slapstick distortions of reality, Disney animators sought more realism in their characters. To accomplish this they incorporated three acting principles of live theater: secondary action, anticipation, and timing. A secondary action is one used after a primary action. For example, if a character falls on its face, that is a primary action. When it gets up, it might engage in a secondary action, such as wiping mud from the face, spitting out dirt, clenching fists, or shaking the head. These secondary actions can be used to show anger, mortification, astonishment, or embarrassment.

Anticipation gives the audience an idea of what is going to happen next. For example, a character with his foot in the air will probably take off running. Anticipation might be used to misdirect the attention of the audience. For example, the character might look to the left and be hit with an object coming from the right.

Timing, which is referred to as acting in live-action films, is also a crucial element in animation. To appear lifelike, animated characters need to have a natural rhythm while walking, running, gesturing, and making other movements. In order to improve their timing, Disney animators studied acting and closely observed actors in movies. They also watched films of cows chewing grass, bears catching salmon in a stream, and acrobats swinging through the air on trapezes. These studies resulted in gestures and timing so perfect that the characters ceased to exist as drawings; audiences accepted them as living individuals.

Snow White

The *Silly Symphony* cartoons served as a platform for audiences to see the animation techniques developed at Disney Studios. Seven of the cartoons, with their believable characters, complex stories, and bright Technicolor hues, won Academy Awards for Best Short Subject (Cartoons) during the 1930s. These include *Three Little Pigs*, *The Tortoise and the Hare*, and *Three Orphan Kittens*.

Despite the success of Mickey Mouse and the *Silly Symphonies*, Disney was eager to break new ground by producing a full-length animated film, something no one had ever done. Disney understood that a ninety-minute cartoon would be unwatchable unless characters expressed complex emotions and extremely lifelike actions. Disney began production on the first full-length animated movie, *Snow White and the Seven Dwarfs*, in 1935.

Disney wanted Snow White to look like a truly realistic female character. As Charles Solomon writes, Snow White "had to be appealing, believable and feminine without being stiff, overly cute or

> **Words in Context**
>
> *timing*
> The use of rhythm, tempo, and pauses to enhance comedic or dramatic elements of acting or character animation.

Disney animators continue a practice started in the company's early days: They draw the movements of a costumed actor in preparation for a film. Disney believed that this exercise helped animators create more natural rhythm, timing, and gestures in their characters.

cartoony."[24] In order to produce a graceful leading lady, animator Hamilton Luske filmed a young dancer dressed in a Snow White costume. She performed various actions and scenes that were first illustrated on storyboards. These included running, stretching, and even singing along with songs from the film. Animators used the films as reference guides to caricature the dancer's actions and make Snow White appear human.

In a departure from the original fairy tale, which was written in 1808 by Jacob and Wilhelm Grimm, Disney wanted to portray the

Training Animators at Disney Studios

When animators were hired for the in-between department at Walt Disney Studios in the mid-1930s, they were expected to attend art classes given by the painter and animator Don Graham. Animation scholar Michael Barrier describes the Disney training program:

[The] hiring and training of inbetweeners became entwined with Don Graham's classes. . . . [It] had become standard practice to interrupt production work for an hour or so in the morning while all the inbetweeners drew from a model. Of Graham's three days a week at the studio, he spent one day with Walt Disney and the directors . . . but he spent two days taking junior members of the staff on sketching expeditions to the Los Angeles Zoo.

By 1935, the inbetween department had metamorphosed into a full-fledged training department. . . . As Graham described the process many years later, each "class" of the dozen or so new hires got 6 to 8 weeks of instruction in drawing and animation before settling into production work; they were encouraged to attend evening classes which by then were held five nights a week.

Michael Barrier, *Hollywood Cartoons*. New York: Oxford University Press, 1999, pp. 139–40.

story's other main characters—the seven dwarfs—as unthreatening and lovable. He also wanted each dwarf to have a unique personality, look, and style. One of the ways Disney accomplished this was to give each dwarf a name that helped animators create seven unique characters. The original pool of about fifty possible names included Jumpy, Deafy, Wheezy, Baldy, Sniffy, and Burpy. Disney eventually settled on Grumpy, Sleepy, Happy, Sneezy, Bashful, Doc, and Dopey and then animators created personalities to match the names. For example, Grumpy had a big red nose, a barrel chest, and often frowned with one eye shut. Dopey, the youngest dwarf, was the only one without a beard. And Dopey was constantly tripping over his baggy clothes.

Adding a Third Dimension

Disney planned to add an extra element of realism to *Snow White* with a new filming process. The multiplane camera, perfected by Iwerks around 1935, created an illusion of depth, or a three-dimensional (3-D) effect. The multiplane looked like a huge bunk bed, with corner posts holding up to five horizontal glass surfaces that could be moved up and down at very precise increments.

The two horizontal surfaces closest to the camera held basic animation cels that depicted character movements. The next two levels were used to hold various elements of a scene's background. The bottom, unmovable plane supplied unchanging background scenery such as trees, fields, clouds, the moon, or sky. Each surface was individually lit with varying levels of light. This added an extra dimension of reality since some areas were brighter than others, much as scenes in a live-action film. A camera was mounted above all the surfaces, more than 15 feet (4.6 m) off the ground. It filmed downward through the multiple glass planes.

The multiplane camera was bulky, expensive to build, and incredibly time-consuming to operate. However, the effects were like none other seen at the time. The camera enabled the animators to create realistic 3-D environments for characters to move through. For example, when Snow White approaches a dark, menacing forest early in the film, she appears to run into and through the woods while the camera seems to follow behind her.

When *Snow White and the Seven Dwarfs* premiered in 1937, it set attendance records and went on to earn $8 million within a year. And according to Solomon, "The success of . . . [*Snow White*] made it one

Words in Context

Technicolor
A full-color filmmaking process renowned for producing strong, saturated colors, first used in animated shorts by Walt Disney in 1932.

of the most significant films in the history of animation. 'Snow White' established the basic pattern for almost every subsequent American animated feature, and its influence can be seen in films made decades later."[25]

Fantasia

Drawing on the unique animation and production techniques that made *Snow White* so successful, Disney produced a string of successful cartoons considered classics today. These include *Pinocchio* (1940), *Bambi* (1942), *Alice in Wonderland* (1951), and *Peter Pan* (1953). Of all the Disney films produced during this era, perhaps none were as artistically ambitious as the two-hour film *Fantasia* (1940), which featured more than five hundred separate animated characters. In modern terms *Fantasia* might be viewed as a series of seven animated music videos set to some of the most sophisticated classical music ever written, including Tchaikovsky's *The Nutcracker* and Stravinsky's *The Rite of Spring*.

Visually, *Fantasia* moves between the awe-inspiring and the humorously absurd. The first piece, *Toccata and Fugue in D Minor*, was created by the sixty animators in Disney's special effects department. They created a beautiful abstract animation of dense blues, reds, purples, and oranges inspired by fireworks, sun bolts, and shooting stars.

Fantasia's third scene, *The Sorcerer's Apprentice*, showcases Mickey Mouse and is perhaps the most memorable scene in the film. Mickey is a young apprentice magician who borrows the magic hat of his teacher, the Great Wizard. With the powers bestowed on him by the hat, Mickey brings a broom to life and puts it work carrying water buckets up and down a flight of stairs to fill a large vat. The broom carries so much water into the workshop that it floods. Mickey chops the broom into pieces, but each wooden sliver comes to life, grows into a new broom, and begins carrying its own buckets of water. The wizard's workshop quickly becomes a flooded disaster. The wizard finally returns and uses his magic powers to make the waters recede.

The Sorcerer's Apprentice exemplifies the expert balance between comedy, cuteness, and incredible animation that is the hallmark of *Fantasia*. It is easy to understand Mickey's popularity when viewing his lovable, humanlike features and gestures. But Disney artists set a

Mickey Mouse conjures a brilliant array of stars and starbursts in *The Sorcerer's Apprentice*, a segment of the 1940 animated spectacular *Fantasia*. The film fused drawing, motion, choreography, sound, and color into a true art form.

new standard for animation that few have equaled with their portrayal of the dancing brooms, the swirling waters, and stars zooming across the Milky Way. According to Solomon, *Fantasia* was "Walt Disney's grand attempt to establish animation as a legitimate art form that fused drawing, motion, design, choreography, sound and color."[26]

Pleased with the outcome, Disney predicted that people would be watching *Fantasia* for decades—and he was right. The work, which required the efforts of more than one thousand artists and technicians, is considered a classic and has been periodically rereleased in theaters over the decades.

Walt Disney died in 1966 at age sixty-five, but the techniques developed by his studio helped to created numerous other animated films. Animated features produced by the corporation now known as the Walt Disney Company had an impact on every decade and every generation. In the 1960s Disney produced *The Jungle Book*; in the 1970s *The Many Adventures of Winnie the Pooh*. The 1980s are remembered for *The Little Mermaid* and the 1990s for *The Lion King*. One of the Walt Disney Company's most recent hits, *Wreck-It Ralph* (2012), earned nearly half a billion dollars. And it all began in 1928 with a funny little mouse named Mickey who sang and danced his way into America's heart.

Chapter Three

Stop-Motion Animation

In the world of animation, the stop-motion technique might be compared to creating moving three-dimensional sculptures. Unlike traditional animators who draw on flat cels, stop-motion animators bring to life objects such as puppets, toys, and models. To create a basic stop-motion film, animators shoot a single frame of an object, move the object slightly by hand, and shoot another frame. When the single shots run continuously in a projector or other video playback system, the object appears to move around the screen with fluid motion.

Stop-motion films use what are known as articulated puppets. In modern stop-motion films, puppets are generally made from fabric, latex rubber, or a nonhardening putty-like clay called plasticine. Articulated puppets are built around a wood or metal skeleton called an armature, which can be moved incrementally after each frame of film is shot.

"A Tedious Process"

Stop-motion animation is very time-consuming. In 1897 veteran cartoonist J. Stuart Blackton and his partner Albert E. Smith created the first-known stop-motion film *Humpty Dumpty Circus* using articulated toy animals and circus performers made from wood. According to Smith, "It was a tedious process in as much as the movement could be achieved only by photographing separately each position."[27]

While there are no existing copies of *Humpty Dumpty Circus*, Blackton's second film, *The Haunted Hotel*, survives and can be seen today on the Internet. The one-minute film, made in 1907, shows a meal being prepared by a set of invisible hands. A knife cuts a loaf of bread, and the slices move around the table before arranging themselves on a plate. A pot lifts itself up and pours coffee into a cup. Oddly, a tiny clown climbs out of a milk pitcher and smokes a corncob pipe as it struts around the table. At the time of its release, *The Haunted Hotel* was popular with audiences, who had never seen such illusions.

> **Words in Context**
>
> *plasticine*
> A nondrying modeling clay made primarily from petroleum jelly, steric acid from beef tallow, and calcium carbonate found in seashells.

"Authentic Film of Prehistoric Life"

The success of *The Haunted Hotel* influenced the creation of other stop-motion shorts. However, the 1925 release of *The Lost World* marked the first successful mix of live-action and stop-motion animation. The silent film was released by First National Pictures, the biggest Hollywood studio of the era. *The Lost World* is about an expedition lost deep in the jungles of Venezuela. The explorers stumble upon rampaging dinosaurs. In one scene an allosaurus viciously attacks a triceratops; in another a tyrannosaurus jumps on top of a brontosaurus.

The dinosaurs in *The Lost World* were created by Willis O'Brien, a stop-motion animation pioneer. O'Brien's partner, sculptor and model maker Marcel Delgado, created innovative new techniques for bringing the dinosaurs to life. Rather than use clay, which was difficult to move between shots, Delgado built fifty dinosaur models with complex skeletons made from aluminum. On top he layered on a web of foam rubber, sponge, and cotton to simulate muscles. The bodies were finally covered with "skins" made from latex rubber. In order to add an extra element of realism, the model builders inserted rubber bladders with extended tubes inside the models. The dinosaurs appeared to be breathing when the bladders were inflated and deflated by off-camera puppeteers blowing into the tubes.

Despite the best efforts of O'Brien and Delgado, the dinosaurs look slightly stilted and choppy on film. However, as Aardman Animations founder Peter Lord and arts journalist Brian Sibley explain, "The animation, by today's standards, was crude but to an audience in the mid-twenties, it appeared so authentic that . . . many observers were convinced they were looking at authentic film of prehistoric life."[28]

Creating King Kong

The most famous work by O'Brien and Delgado can be seen in the groundbreaking classic *King Kong*, released in 1933. The one-hundred-minute story follows a filmmaker and his lovely assistant Ann Darrow, played by actress Fay Wray, who travel to the mysterious Skull Island. They discover a gigantic gorilla, King Kong, and watch in fright as he battles various dinosaurs. The filmmaker captures King Kong and transports him to Manhattan. The gorilla breaks free, kidnaps Darrow, and climbs the Empire State Building. Finally, King Kong is shot down by fighter planes.

The producers of *King Kong* hired O'Brien and Delgado to create the gorilla. While in the movie it was estimated to be 50 feet (15 m) tall, the gorilla model crafted by O'Brien and Delgado was actually 18 inches (46 cm) high. The animators built King Kong from rubber and rabbit fur molded over a metal skeleton. For close-ups, O'Brien and Delgado created a full-scale hand large enough to hold Wray. In addition, a 20-foot (6 m) model of Kong's head and shoulders was sculpted from rubber and covered with bear hides. The full-scale version of Kong was built with wires in the mouth and face. These could be manipulated to express a wide range of human emotions in Kong, including happiness, rage, and confusion. These expressions prompted audiences to feel fear, joy, and sympathy for King Kong and to view the creature as much more than an animated puppet.

To make sure the stop-motion scenes had a strong element of realism, the animators visited zoos to watch gorillas in action. They even attended wrestling matches to better coordinate the character's body movements when he wrestled dinosaurs. O'Brien also invented a unique way to add a 3-D element to *King Kong*. He had several layers of 8 by 10 foot (2.4 by 3 m) sheet glass painted with jungle scenes. The animation stand, where the models were filmed in stop-motion action, was sandwiched between the sheets of glass. When the scenes were filmed, the painted glass was placed in front of, next to, and behind the animated creatures, providing a sense of depth.

Once O'Brien filmed the scenes with the King Kong models, he mixed the stop-motion action with performances by live actors. The finished filmed scenes were rear-projected onto a clear screen as actors performed in front of it. For example, one scene featured King Kong fighting a life-and-death battle with a tyrannosaurus. This scene was rear-projected onto a screen with Wray acting in front. As a movie camera filmed both Wray and the stop-motion sequence together, the actress lay in the crook of a tree screaming in fright as the beasts appeared to battle behind her.

O'Brien's techniques allowed actors, for the first time, to react to stop-motion creatures. This brought stop-motion animation new

The metal skeleton used to create the gorilla model for the original 1933 *King Kong* movie was only eighteen inches tall. The animators built King Kong from rubber and rabbit fur molded over the metal skeleton (pictured).

respect, as renowned animator Ray Harryhausen explains: "In *King Kong* . . . the creatures (certainly Kong) were so well integrated with the live action that the animation was the star of the picture."[29]

When *King Kong* was released in March 1933, crowds in New York lined up around the block to buy tickets for each of the ten daily showings, which sold out for days. The film was so successful that it was rereleased in 1938, 1942, 1946, and 1952.

"The End of an Era"

Harryhausen was only thirteen years old when *King Kong* was released, but the film made a big impression on him. Harryhausen saw the movie several times and began experimenting with stop-motion animation shorts. In one early effort, a clay monster attacks Harryhausen's dog. By the time Harryhausen was twenty, he was building articulated dinosaurs and making latex rubber monster masks. He explains his motivation: "It was now clear to me that stop-motion model animation offered me the best opportunities for making a name for myself and earning a living from the work that I most enjoyed."[30]

Words in Context
animation stand
A flat surface that acts as a stage for models and scenery during the filming of stop-motion sequences.

Harryhausen got his first break in show business in 1947 when he was hired as a technician to work with O'Brien and Delgado on *Mighty Joe Young*, the sequel to *King Kong*. Like *King Kong*, *Mighty Joe Young* combined live-action and stop-motion animation sequences of a giant gorilla (Joe Young). The film's final scenes represented a leap forward in the art of stop-motion animation. In one scene Joe Young rescues several children trapped on the roof of a burning orphanage. The burning orphanage rescue helped *Mighty Joe Young* win the Academy Award for Best Visual Effects in 1950, a category that did not exist when *King Kong* was produced.

Harryhausen did 90 percent of the stop-motion animation on *Mighty Joe Young*, and when it was released in 1948 it was a hit. However, as Harryhausen writes, "*Mighty Joe Young* was the last picture of

its kind. It was the end of an era for such expensive effects features. . . .
I had to find a way of producing screen adventures in a more practical
and affordable manner."[31]

The Dynamation Dreamscape

Searching for a way to produce cheaper stop-motion special effects,
Harryhausen turned to a technique he first developed in 1939. Rather
than use expensive glass set paintings like O'Brien, Harryhausen invented a method he called Dynamation. This was first used in 1952 to
produce *The Beast from 20,000 Fathoms*.

Dynamation is also known as a split-screen technique. The screen
is split in two, with the live action typically appearing on the lower
third of the screen while the stop-motion action and scenery appear
on the upper two-thirds of the screen. This technique enables animated models and live actors to be on-screen together.

Dynamation involves running the film
through the camera twice, also known as
double-exposure. On the first pass, the
stop-motion action is shot in the top two-
thirds of the film frame. The film is then rewound. On the second pass, live actors are
filmed in the bottom third of the frame performing their reactions to the stop-motion
monsters. As Harryhausen explains, "The end result is that all three
elements—the lower and top sections of the screen and the animated
model or models—are seen as one, so giving the illusion of a huge
beast being actually part of the live-action."[32]

Dynamation required extremely precise coordination between
projectors, cameras, models, lighting, and other elements. Harryhausen developed and executed all of the film and model work himself. Audiences were unaware of Harryhausen's complex technical
achievements, because his Dynamation split-screen scenes were considered seamless for the era.

Harryhausen produced numerous films with Dynamation and
other special effects techniques he developed. These include *Earth vs.
the Flying Saucers* (1956), *Jason and the Argonauts* (1963), *One Million*

> **Words in Context**
> *articulated*
> Two or more sections
> of a puppet connected
> by a flexible joint.

Ray Harryhausen, Stop-Motion Magician

Ray Harryhausen was born in Los Angeles on June 29, 1920. A child with an artistic streak, he spent his time drawing, painting, and making puppets and marionettes. At the age of five Harryhausen saw *The Lost World*, the first film that mixed live-action with stop-motion creatures including dinosaurs. Entranced by the on-screen images, Harryhausen developed a life-long fascination with dinosaurs.

Several years later, at the age of thirteen, Harryhausen saw the stop-motion classic *King Kong*. That film, he later said, changed his life. He began putting on puppet shows with characters modeled after the enormous gorilla monster and became fixated on the mechanics of the stop-motion animation process. By the time he was eighteen Harryhausen was designing and building sets and models for his own stop-motion animation experiments. Those efforts helped him land a job working on the 1949 stop-motion film *Mighty Joe Young*. The work he did on that film helped launch his career.

Between the 1950s and the early 1980s Harryhausen created an array of terrifying and memorable movie creatures including dinosaurs, a six-legged octopus, skeleton warriors, a Cyclops, a six-armed goddess wielding a sword in each hand, and a snake-haired Medusa-like monster. His creatures were created with the help of a stop-motion technique he devised called Dynamation.

Harryhausen retired in 1984 but his work influenced a generation of filmmakers including Steven Spielberg, James Cameron, and George Lucas. Ray Harryhausen died on May 7, 2013 at the age of ninety-two.

Dynamation

Ray Harryhausen's Dynamation technique provided a cheaper, faster way to create realistic, synchronized interaction between miniature models and live actors. For a scene that showed people fleeing in panic as a dinosaur walked out from behind a building toward a busy intersection, the technique worked like this:

Background for the scene, including actors running toward the camera, was filmed on a city street. The first frame of the scene was then projected onto a translucent rear projection screen. On this type of screen, the image appears on the front of the screen when illuminated by a projector from the rear.

A motion picture camera was placed opposite the projector and on the other side of the screen so that the film clip could be re-photographed as it was projected onto the screen. A large glass sheet, or matte glass, was placed between the camera and the screen and a dinosaur model was placed on a table between the glass and the screen. The artist blacked out the lower portion of the glass and repositioned the dinosaur each time the film in the projector advanced a frame. The dinosaur appeared in each frame, with only the scenery behind it visible. Next, the projector and camera were rewound. The artist replaced the glass sheet; this time the upper portion was blacked out. The table and model were removed and the film re-shot. This time only objects and scenery in the foreground would be visible on film.

When the images were combined, the dinosaur appeared to step out from behind a building, stalking toward terrified people running for their lives.

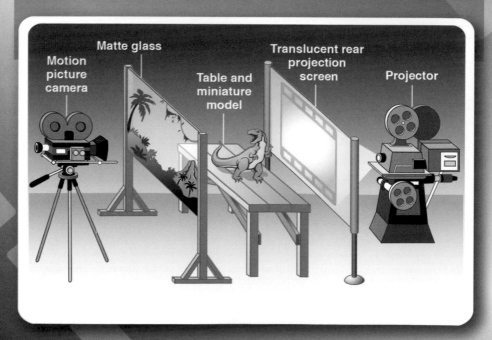

Years B.C. (1966), *The Golden Voyage of Sinbad* (1973), and *Clash of the Titans* (1981).

When Harryhausen died in May 2013 at age ninety-two, he was lauded by the world's top animation and special effects directors. According to *Avatar* producer James Cameron, "I think all of us who are practitioners in the arts of science fiction and fantasy movies now all feel that we're standing on the shoulders of a giant. If not for Ray's contribution to the collective dreamscape, we wouldn't be who we are."[33]

Will Vinton's Claymation

While dozens of directors imitated Harryhausen's Dynamation special effects methods, there were few successful feature films that were solely stop-motion animation. The technique was seen on Saturday morning children's TV shows like *Gumby*, which ran from 1955 to 1970. But Hollywood producers did not think full-length stop-motion feature films would appeal to adults. However, attitudes began to change in the mid-1970s. During this period many young stop-motion artists, including Will Vinton, Nick Park, and Tim Burton, were experimenting with adult oriented themes and social commentary.

Vinton's stop-motion animations were created entirely from clay, leading him to coin the term *Claymation* to describe his work. His technique differed from the work of other stop-motion animators, whose characters and scenes were crafted from clay and other materials such as cloth, cardboard, wood, and plastic. Using only clay, Vinton's characters, sets, and props provided a 3-D look unique for the times. This 3-D look would not be duplicated until the 1990s with the advent of advanced computer animation.

Vinton's most ambitious film was produced with sculptor Bob Gardiner in 1985. At eighty-six minutes, *The Adventures of Mark Twain* was the first full-length Claymation feature ever made. The film tells the story of the celebrated writer Mark Twain as he travels the world in a fantastic airship. Twain is hoping to see Halley's comet, which streaks through the sky once every seventy-five years. Every single part of *Mark Twain*, including characters, sets, bodies of water, and even the sky, was made entirely from clay.

Film reviewer Ian Drury describes the Claymation in *The Adventures of Mark Twain*:

> For 1985, the stop motion claymation is fantastic. The clay characters are all highly expressive and expertly designed, and every scene features a boundless look of creativity and color. The animation of water and the motion of the sky are reminiscent of something out of a Vincent van Gogh painting. . . . [Vinton] captures such a high range of emotions in the faces of his characters, particularly in the face of Mark Twain.[34]

Wallace and Gromit

In England Nick Park was another stop-motion clay animator whose work appealed to both adults and children. Park began work on the renowned clay animation *Wallace and Gromit: A Grand Day Out* when he was a twenty-four-year-old student in 1982. *A Grand Day Out* follows an absent-minded inventor, Wallace, and his dog, Gromit, as they build a rocket ship and travel to the moon in search of cheese.

When Park began shooting *A Grand Day Out*, he expected the project to take one or two years. However, he soon discovered why Albert E. Smith had long ago called stop-motion animation a "tedious process." A single written paragraph of the script, in which Wallace and Gromit build a rocket ship, took Park eighteen months to film.

In 1985 Park decided he needed help. He went to work for Aardman Animations in Bristol, England, making commercials and music videos such as the famed stop-motion classic "Sledgehammer" by Peter Gabriel. In between the commercial work, Aardman animators helped Park finish *A Grand Day Out*. However, even with assistants and the use of a professional studio, Park was only able to produce one and a half to three seconds of animation each day. By the time *A Grand Day Out* was finished in 1989, it had been in production for nearly seven years.

Park's hard work paid off. When *A Grand Day Out* was released, audiences fell in love with Wallace and Gromit. While the round, squishy characters with oddly proportioned features do not look re-

An artist builds a model of a character that appears in a scene from one of the *Wallace and Gromit* animated films. In stop-motion animation, artists create multiple models of each character so that scenes can be shot simultaneously on different sets.

alistic, Park's clay work allows them to convey ideas and emotions as though they were alive. And although Wallace does not say much—and Gromit makes no sound at all—audiences know exactly what they are thinking in every scene. This is due to the remarkably expressive eyes and mouths of Park's clay characters. He turns lumps of clay into seemingly living, breathing beings that audiences care about and enjoy.

A Grand Day Out was followed by several more Wallace and Gromit clay adventures, including *The Wrong Trousers* (1993), *A Close Shave* (1995), and the full-length feature *The Curse of the Were-Rabbit* (2005). The latter three films each won Academy Awards. Park also made *Chicken Run* in 2000, which did not feature Wallace or Gromit.

Making *Corpse Bride* Characters

Animators working on the animated film *Corpse Bride* in 2005 built characters with internal gearboxes that could be moved by turning a small hex wrench called an Allen key. *Corpse Bride* puppet fabrication supervisor Graham G. Maiden explains:

We managed to get a gearing system the size of a small orange and have it accessible through the back of the head. Paddles and strings with fixing points within the skin were attached to the gearing system. This allowed us to manipulate the puppet's expressions. The puppet of Victoria, for example, has a hole in her bow in her hair and also in her ears, as does Corpse Bride and Victor. You access the gearing system with an Allen key and turn the gears that open and close her mouth, that way they can make her smile or pout. The heads also have paddles in them to make the eyebrow raise or fall so they can either look surprised, angry or serious.

Quoted in Ron Barbagallo, "Tim Burton's Corpse Bride," Animation Conservation, 2005. www.animationartconservation.com.

Chicken Run was the most successful stop-motion animation feature in history. It cost $45 million to make and brought in nearly $225 million worldwide.

Although creating stop-motion films is extremely difficult and time-consuming, it was worth the trouble to Park, who describes the wonders of clay animation: "Everybody knows what a lump of clay is and seeing it come to life is quite a magical thing. You can see the material and see it moving and suddenly gaining a character somehow."[35]

"It's Just Something Magical"

There is little doubt that stop-motion animation features will be made as long as there are animators to make them. In 2005 Tim Burton explained his attraction to stop-motion after directing *Corpse Bride*, a stop-motion animated fantasy film set in a fictional Victorian-era village in Europe: "The artists and the animators are . . . in a dark room for two years making these things come to life. It's [an] art form that is unlike anything else. You watch something and it might've taken an animator a week to shoot, depending on the complexity, and when you see it, it's just something magical."[36]

Chapter Four

Computer-Generated Animation

For more than a decade, writer-director James Cameron immersed himself in the task of inventing an entirely new world for the big screen. The result was the epic 2009 science fiction–action film *Avatar*, a marvel of 3-D computer-generated imagery (CGI) and live action. The film's artistically ambitious animated sequences blended seamlessly with the actions of live actors in a tale of the fictional planet of Pandora—home to extraordinary beings called the Na'vi. The aliens lived in a natural world that combined elements of Earth with the startling beauty of an otherworldly paradise. The conflict in the story involved humans who were overrunning Pandora in search of a rare mineral found only there.

A Living World of Light

While in the planning stages of *Avatar*, Cameron traveled the world's oceans in a small, personal submarine—taking notes and making sketches. He drew pictures of the sea creatures that swam past his portholes. These included bioluminescent fish, which glowed with pulsating light as they moved through the inky darkness.

Cameron's undersea visions were incorporated directly into the *Avatar* script. His notes included descriptions such as "a glowing phantasmagorical [eerily bizarre] forest, purple moss reacts to pressure, rings of green light, ripples on the pond expand outward from each footfall, exploding rings of light where his feet touch down. Dreamlike, surreal beauty."[37]

When filming began on *Avatar* in 2005, art directors Rob Stromberg and Dylan Cole created special effects with CGI based on Cameron's descriptions of color and light. As film journalist Lisa Fitzpatrick explains, "The bioluminescent light patterns were woven into all the living creatures on Pandora, including the planet herself. One goal of this effort was to inspire the audience to see these light patterns as a living network, a nervous system of sorts, that connects everyone and everything to one another."[38]

CGI has been used in films since the late 1970s. But Cameron and his crew of technicians, artists, and computer wizards developed their own unique 3-D animated special effects, more advanced than any seen before. This enabled them to capture on film what had existed only in Cameron's imagination. As *The Lord of the Rings* director Peter Jackson explains, "Cameron has created a mind-boggling beautiful, dangerous, alternate reality that has never been seen before on screen."[39]

Whitney's Gun Directors

The CGI animation of *Avatar* presents lifelike characters that earlier generations of animators could only have dreamed of. The earliest computer animation, done in the late 1950s, relied on big, slow machines that had (by modern standards) limited capabilities. Early computers were largely designed for accounting and other business purposes, not creating art. No drawing or painting software existed and the machines were not sophisticated enough to create complex digital images of people, creatures, objects, or animals. The first images produced on computers consisted of repeating geometric shapes, pulsating patterns, and swirling dots.

To compensate for the limitations of early computers, special effects filmmaker John Whitney Sr. went to great lengths to produce some of the first CGI. In 1958 Whitney built a computer system from World War II–era antiaircraft gun directors. The 12-foot (3.7 m) high machines were very primitive analog computers built to aim guns at enemy aircraft. Soldiers programmed the machines by feeding in basic information like target speed and distance. Whitney modified the gun directors to move lights and cameras around in preprogrammed patterns. Digital arts journalist Kevin Holmes explains: "The custom-

James Cameron's 2009 film *Avatar* took 3-D animation to new heights. In the movie's magnificent imaginary world, animated sequences blended seamlessly with the actions of live actors.

ized gun was able to control cameras that would maneuver above the artwork and, astoundingly, perform the kinds of functions that would later be common on digital computers. . . . [While] his machines were mechanical, they anticipated the applications of computer software which we now take for granted."[40]

"A Legitimate Medium for Art"

Whitney used his machines to create experimental animated shorts that were compiled into the seven-minute film *Catalog* (1961). The movie begins with the title and the year pictured on the screen. The words and letters blur and then refocus as interwoven circular patterns similar to those created by the geometric drawing toy Spirograph. The patterns morph into intertwining waves of bright pinks, yellows, and oranges which then become pulsating dots, swirling circles, spinning stars, and more.

Whitney's work caught the attention of executives at IBM, then the world's leading computer maker. Long before the advent of PCs and laptops, IBM made computers for large corporations such as airlines, banks, and electric utilities. A typical mid-1960s IBM computer weighed 1,700 pounds (771 kg), was bigger than an automobile, and cost around $125,000.

Despite the size and cost of the machines, IBM hoped to convince the world that its computers could be used for many purposes including art and animation. To that end, IBM created an artist-in-residence program in 1965 and hired Whitney as its first artist. Whitney's first film at IBM, *Permutations* (1966), consisted of 281 colorful dots moving in a graceful, rhythmic pattern. Whitney explained the significance of *Permutations*: "[It] would be difficult to find a better demonstration of the powers of the computer as an animation tool than this film sequence. Imagine having to animate by hand 281 points, all moving in precise orbits at independent rates and directions."[41]

In 1975 Whitney released *Arabesque*, a seven-minute short with swirling psychedelic colors. *Arabesque* is considered today as a seminal computer-generated film. According to the filmmaker's website, "John Whitney had balanced science with aesthetics [beauty], and defined the computer as a legitimate medium for art."[42]

Animated *Death Star*

On *Arabesque* Whitney collaborated with animator Larry Cuba, a widely recognized pioneer in the use of computers in animation art. Around the time of *Arabesque*'s release, Cuba showed one of his own CGI art films to George Lucas, who was in the process of building the visual effects company Industrial Light & Magic (ILM). Impressed with the film, Lucas hired Cuba to work on the first *Star Wars* movie. Released in 1977, *Star Wars Episode IV: A New Hope* contained a Cuba-created computer animation that reveals the plans for the *Death Star* battle station, seen as a hologram projected from the robot R2D2's memory. This scene spells out to the characters with primitive graphics how the plot will be carried out. Computer-generated animation was not advanced enough at the time to replace actors, sets, or costuming. However, within a few years, CGI techniques were developed to the point that the digital images could be used for more advanced visual manipulation.

In 1982 Disney released *Tron*, the first film with an entirely computer-generated world, complete with humans. About twenty minutes of *Tron* is CGI, and the most famous scene, the Lightcycle race, shows motorcycle-type vehicles zooming across the screen. Although the scene looks cartoonish, the faces of the Lightcycle riders have realistic, computer-generated human features.

In the years since *Tron*, CGI has been used for animated special effects sequences in numerous ILM blockbusters, including the *Indiana Jones* series, the *Harry Potter* series, the *Jurassic Park* series, and the *Back to the Future* trilogy. Filmmakers at ILM have integrated animation techniques both old and new in the creation of memorable scenes. They melded digital creations, stop-motion animation, and small-scale miniature sets. They also made broad use of animatronics, that is, robotic machines shaped into dinosaurs, space monsters, and other characters.

A human character in the 1982 movie *Tron* rides a computer-generated lightcycle through a world that was also created entirely on a computer. Computer-generated images, or CGI, have been used for animated special effects sequences in numerous other popular films.

Digitizing Clay Models

The CGI department of ILM evolved into Pixar Animation Studios in 1986. One of the first computer-animated films to come out of the studio was *Luxo Jr.*, a two-minute animation featuring two hopping desk lamps, one large and one small. Its creator, former Disney animator John Lasseter, combined computer graphics with classic Disney animation principles such as anticipation, secondary action, and timing. In the film the two lamps play a game of catch with an inflated ball, but the smaller lamp, Luxo Jr., bounces on top of the ball until it pops. Luxo Jr. soon appears with another, bigger ball. In a remarkable feat of computer animation, the lamps clearly express feelings such as dejection and joy through their simple movements.

> **Words in Context**
> *animatronics*
> Lifelike robots created with electronics and mechanical parts; used by filmmakers in special effects scenes to mimic mythical creatures, plants, and animals such as dinosaurs.

Lasseter's talents went far beyond animating lamps, however. In 1991 he began work on an eighty-minute computer-animated feature film about toys that come to life. The result, *Toy Story*, was created by a team of twenty-eight animators and more than eighty production people. *Toy Story* follows the adventures of two toys, a space ranger named Buzz Lightyear and his rival Woody, a likeable cowboy. No cels were used in the creation of *Toy Story*, but like all animated films, production required thousands of old-fashioned drawings before filming could begin. Animators created detailed sketches of every character, animal, toy, vehicle, room, and outdoor scene. Each character drawing was turned into a clay model much like those used in stop-motion animation. Animators moved a tool called a digitizer wand over every part of every model. Connected to a computer, the wand created 3-D digital versions of the characters.

Dimensions in Computer Animation

While Disney and other traditional animators added depth by shooting on multiplane cameras, *Toy Story* animators created a 3-D effect with digitizer wands and software that placed 3-D objects on what is

Pixar's *Luxo Jr.*

One of the first animated films produced at Pixar, *Luxo Jr.*, was directed by John Lasseter in 1986. The computer-animated short features two unlikely characters, a large and small desk lamp, playing with a small ball. The large "older" lamp, Luxo, was what Lasseter conceived as a patient father looking on as his son, a smaller lamp named Luxo Jr., jumps on the ball until it breaks. After a moment of sadness, represented by the small desk lamp hanging its lamp shade "head," Luxo Jr. finds a new ball ten times as big.

When *Luxo Jr.* was released, it was hailed as the computer graphics *Steamboat Willie*, a film that represented an animation breakthrough. And critics praised the remarkable level of emotion conveyed by inanimate objects. The Pixar website explains how *Luxo Jr.* came to be: "When John Lasseter was learning how to make models, he chose the nearest, easiest subject: an architect's lamp sitting on his desk. He started moving it around in the animation system like it was alive, and it eventually became a Pixar short that was nominated for an Academy Award."

Pixar, *Luxo Jr.*, 2012. www.pixar.com.

called a three-axis coordinate system. Each dimension is represented by the letters x, y, or z. Like lines on a sheet of graph paper, the x axis is horizontal and the y axis is vertical. With the addition of the z axis, the third dimension—depth—is represented.

When creating *Toy Story* the digitizer wand provided data called animation variables, or avars, to the computer. An avar is a single control point that represents a specific set of x-y-z coordinates. When an animator moves an avar, the software changes the features of the model. For example, Woody had more than 700 avars, with 212 in the face alone. These were manipulated on the computer to change facial features, body and limb movements, and the lips and tongue for speaking parts.

Toy Story had four hundred characters that were nearly as complex as Woody. Once the models and all the details were fed into computers, animators used painting and inking tools in the software programs to add flesh tones, clothes, hairstyles, and other details. The trees in exterior scenes had more than 1 million leaves, which had the ability to shimmer in the wind, reflect light and shadows, and fall to the ground. The human boy in the film had more than ten thousand individual hairs growing on his head. A 1996 article by journalist Michael Salinders describes this animation process as vexingly slow: "At top speed, Pixar could produce only about 3½ minutes of complete animation each week. For nine months, technicians and animators trained their talents on one critical point, the color and texture of a [child's] hair. This element is still remembered as one of the toughest single parts of *Toy Story*."[43]

Although it took four years to complete, the hard work paid off when *Toy Story* was released in 1995. The film received an Academy Award nomination and went on to earn nearly $382 million.

> **Words in Context**
> *avars*
> Short for "animation variables," avars are control points on a 3-D animated character that can be manipulated to move the body, limbs, and facial features.

Motion Capture

The creation of *Toy Story* was a long, complicated process, made even more time-consuming by the slow computers of the era. However, computer speed and software power increased dramatically in the early 2000s. With improved machines, animators were able to use a new technique called motion capture (or performance capture). In a sense, motion capture is the high-tech version of rotoscoping, the use of live actors to create frame-by-frame depictions of animated characters. In the digital version of rotoscoping, computers record movements of actors and turn them into 3-D models.

In recent years motion capture has been used in numerous animated films, including *Shrek*, *Shrek 2*, and *The Polar Express*. The technique was made famous in the 2002 live-action film *The Lord of the Rings: The Two Towers*. In that film the character Gollum is a computer-generated digital animation inserted into the live action. Gollum was created from the movements, facial features, and voice of actor Andy Serkis. To create Gollum, Serkis wore a skintight mocap, or motion capture, suit studded with reflective reference markers and stripes located, like avars, at key points on his body. Cameras were placed around Serkis, and bright lights were shown on the reflectors. Serkis then acted out his part as Gollum, crouching, crawling, cringing, attacking, hissing, and sniffing.

The cameras produced a 3-D digital version of Serkis's movements. This was given to a team of digital animators who used the motion capture data to create key frames, or starting and ending poses for various scenes. Animators were then able to overlay Serkis's im-

Actors wearing motion capture suits studded with reflective reference markers perform the movements that will allow artists to create realistic, digitally animated characters. The scene being shot here is for *The Adventures of Tintin*, a 2011 film directed by Steven Spielberg.

age with a computer-generated animation of Gollum, complete with skeleton and muscle system. As film journalist Brian Sibley explains, the software program imposes "Gollum's proportions onto the capture of Andy's body movements. So, if Andy's arms are shorter than Gollum's, or his thighs larger, then the computer will process those differences and read and interpret the actor's moves in terms of Gollum's physique. Once 'captured,' the Gollum image is then open for modification by the animators."[44]

When *The Lord of the Rings* was made, motion capture was not advanced enough to capture Serkis's facial movements. Gollum's face was completely animated by hand, a laborious process. In 2005 the facial animation process was made easier when Serkis appeared in a remake of *King Kong*. The crew glued reflective markers all over Serkis's face, and the data was used to create digital muscles and facial expressions. However, the reflectors continually fell off under the heat of the movie lights. When James Cameron produced *Avatar* in 2009, he needed to solve the facial reflector problem in order to create hyperrealistic human-alien hybrids.

Crossing the Uncanny Valley

To film *Avatar* Cameron hit on the idea of creating a mocap helmet. He inserted tiny cameras inside a helmet and pointed them at actors' faces. The cameras tracked every facial movement, including darting eyes, furrowed eyebrows, twitching noses, and the complex interactions of teeth, tongue, lips, and jaws. The facial movements of each actor, recorded by the cameras, were digitally transferred to the aliens in the movie. This gave the computer-generated characters the same range of emotions and expressions as the human actors. According to Cameron, "I knew I could not fail if I had a 100 percent closeup of the actor 100 percent of the time that traveled with them wherever they went. That really makes a closeup come alive."[45]

The problem with motion capture is that computer-generated animation of the human face can appear creepy and strange if not

Uncanny Valley

Film critic Anne Thompson explains the major problem experienced by animators who work with computers and robot technology in creating human characters for animated films. The problem is known in the industry as the uncanny valley.

> Audiences are especially sensitive to renderings of the human face, and the closer a digital creation gets to a photorealistic human, the higher expectations get. If you map human movements and expression to cute furry creatures that dance and sing like people, then audiences willingly suspend disbelief and go along with it. But if you try to give a digital character a humanoid face, anything short of perfection can be uncanny—thus the term. Sometimes audience unease is to a character's advantage; in *The Lord of the Rings* the creature Gollum was supposed to be unsettling. But [in *Avatar*] Cameron was looking for empathy.

Anne Thompson, "How James Cameron's Innovative New 3D Tech Created *Avatar*," *Popular Mechanics*, January 2, 2010. www.popularmechanics.com.

done properly. *Uncanny* means "eerie" or "weird," and bad motion capture of the human face is what filmmakers call the uncanny valley. Despite the mocap helmet and other innovations, Cameron's original *Avatar* aliens fell into the uncanny valley. As a result, animators spent a year reworking digital formulas to translate motion capture into humanlike movements and expressions. Once this was done, the *Avatar* aliens appeared startlingly realistic. The complex technology and motion capture animation blended seamlessly into the story, and viewers were able to lose themselves in *Avatar*'s fantasy world. With earnings of $2.7 billion, *Avatar* became the highest-grossing film of all time. By 2013 Cameron was making plans for two *Avatar* sequels.

Digital Tools of the Trade

Computer-generated animation will continue to advance. Computers might someday even produce animated performers so realistic that they replace live actors. However, 3-D modeling software and mocap suits are simply sophisticated tools used by animators to tell a good story. Countless animators are using those and other tools of their art to create stories to entertain future generations.

Chapter Five

Anime

In Japan animation is called anime, and there are several parallels between Japanese and American animated films. Many popular animated characters in both countries were first seen in comic books, known as manga in Japan. And like American animators, Japanese animators have been strongly influenced over the years by the full-length features produced by Walt Disney Studios.

While there are similarities, the artistic look of anime can vary greatly from the animation produced in the United States. The backgrounds in American animation tend to be stationary while the characters move around the screen, often in nonstop action. Anime often looks as if it was shot with a handheld camera. An unmoving character may be shown from various angles while the scenery shifts behind it. Renowned anime artist Hayao Miyazaki calls this technique gratuitous motion; instead of every character in constant motion, people might just sit for a moment, sigh, or gaze at a trickling stream. This does not advance the story but provides insight into the character's thoughts or feelings. According to Miyazaki, "We have a word for [gratuitous motion] in Japanese. It's called 'ma.' Emptiness. It's there intentionally. . . . If you just have non-stop action with no breathing space at all, it's just busyness."[46]

Art from Ancient Symbols

The concept of *ma* has its roots in ancient Japanese traditions, which provide numerous symbols incorporated into anime. These symbols, taken from mythology, poetry, historical tales, and religious rites, provide viewers with special emotional clues when incorporated into anime scenes. One of the most commonly used symbols, the cherry blossom, holds a revered place in Japanese tradition. These delicate pink flowers, which bloom in spring, appear repeatedly in anime and present a variety of ideas at once. Cherry blossoms falling on a character might represent the freshness of spring. But because cherry trees only bloom for a short time, the beauty is touched by sadness and can also represent the fleeting quality of life. This is in keeping with the widely held Japanese belief—and another recurring aspect of anime—that romantic love is more meaningful if it is tinged by tragedy.

The supernatural thriller *X/1999* is among many anime stories that use the symbolism of cherry blossoms to signal changes in mood. Whenever the handsome assassin wizard named Seishirō arrives on a scene, he is preceded by cherry blossoms flickering across the screen. After he kills his victims, they become gruesome meals for a beautiful, eternally blossoming cherry tree. In this way viewers can sense both beauty and tragedy embodied by the ancient symbol of the cherry tree.

Cherry blossoms are just one of many flowers used in anime that have symbolic meaning in Japan. Lotus flowers represent purity of body, speech, and mind; anime artists might use them to represent ideal feminine attributes of beauty and grace. Other flowers used by anime artists include peonies, which are associated with happiness and prosperity; roses, which are associated with sensuality; and irises, which are associated with strength, vitality, boldness, and power.

Tezuka's Different Angles

While flowers do not appear in every animated film produced in Japan, they are part of anime's expressive artistic style. Sweeping cinematic effects, with close-ups, rapid zooms, freeze frames, and changing viewpoints are other defining characteristics of anime. The cinematic style was popularized by Osamu Tezuka, one of Japan's most famous animators.

Born in 1928, Tezuka loved the Sunday funnies star Felix the Cat and drew his first comic strip when he was nine years old. By the

1950s Tezuka was writing and drawing extremely long manga stories using a technique he perfected called cinematographic. With this artistic style, comic panels flowed as in a movie, coming to life on the pages. As Tezuka, explains:

> I experimented with close-ups and different angles, and instead of using only one frame for an action scene or the climax (as was customary), I made a point of depicting a movement or facial expression with many frames, even many pages. The result was a super-long comic that ran to 500, 600, even 1,000 pages. I also believed that comics were capable of more than just making people laugh. So in my themes I incorporated tears, grief, anger, and hate, and I created stories where the ending was not always happy.[47]

The Mighty Atom

Tezuka's cinematographic drawing techniques were easily suited to anime. In the late 1950s Tezuka went to work for Toei Animation. Founded in 1948, Toei was Japan's first anime studio. The company found initial success imitating the most popular animated films in the world, including *Cinderella*, *Alice in Wonderland*, *Peter Pan*, and other Walt Disney classics. In 1961 Tezuka founded his own anime studio, Mushi Productions (literally, Bug Productions), named after his favorite creatures, insects. At the time of the studio's founding, Tezuka had been writing a manga called *The Mighty Atom* for nine years. The manga was very successful, and Tezuka wanted to create an anime based on the character. The Mighty Atom was a boy robot with superpowers. He was built by a mad scientist in what was then considered the far distant future, the year 2003.

The space-age Mighty Atom flew through the air using rockets in his feet. He sought out criminals with his searchlight eyes, foiled evil

Words in Context

cinematographic
An artistic style with panels that flow like scenes in a movie; it uses filmmaking techniques such as pans, zooms, and changing viewpoints.

Enormous, saucerlike eyes are a defining characteristic of the Japanese style of animation known as anime. In Japanese art, the eyes are viewed as a window through which the character's emotions and inner thoughts can be viewed.

plots using his computer brain, and fought bad guys with lasers in his hands and a machine gun on his backside. Beneath the Mighty Atom's chest beat a pure heart fueled by a nuclear reactor. The Mighty Atom could understand sixty languages and could smash through solid rock with his 100,000 horsepower strength. Despite his awesome powers, the Mighty Atom was drawn using the "cute and cuddly" formula perfected by Disney. In order to appeal to schoolchildren, the Mighty Atom had a baby face with a tiny nose and small mouth. Tezuka, who was inspired by the 1930s cartoon *Betty Boop*, also drew his character with large, expressive eyes.

The enormous eyes used by Tezuka were imitated by scores of anime artists in later years. This feature is often singled out by Westerners as a defining characteristic of anime. Like cherry blossoms, the eyes have great symbolic importance. As Japanese art and culture expert Mizuki Takahashi explains, large saucerlike eyes demonstrate a character's complex inner thoughts. "[The eyes] serve as mirrors that reflect the character's emotions," says Takahashi. "In other words, the eyes literally are the windows of the soul; by looking at the eyes, [viewers] can intuit the character's feelings, which remain unexpressed in dialog."[48]

Limited Animation

Tezuka had a popular character, but he understood he could not afford to produce an anime in the Disney manner, with twenty-four drawings for every second of film. However, Tezuka found inspiration elsewhere. In 1962 the American cartoon series *The Flintstones* premiered in Japan. Unlike the intricately drawn Disney cartoons, *The Flintstones* was created quickly, with animators using only eight to ten cels per second. This technique, known as planned animation or limited animation, created characters with jerky movements. But planned animation allowed producers to create cartoons quickly, which meant the shows could be broadcast on a weekly basis. After seeing *The Flintstones*, Tezuka found his production model for *The Mighty Atom*.

> **Words in Context**
> *limited animation*
> A method of inexpensive traditional cartoon production that used eight cels per second rather than twenty-four and relied on only three mouth positions for speaking characters.

Besides using a low number of cels per second, *The Mighty Atom* used only three mouth positions for characters: open, shut, and half open. This was unlike Disney cartoons, in which the characters had at least a dozen different mouth movements when they were speaking. Sometimes characters would speak with their backs to the camera, meaning no mouth animation was necessary.

The "God of Anime"

The Mighty Atom debuted on Fuji TV in Japan on January 1, 1963, and was an instant hit. However, the success came with a price. Tezuka's agreement with Fuji TV required him to produce the anime with an extremely low budget on a very tight schedule. This meant the Mushi animators were poorly paid and overworked. As anime expert Simon Richmond explains, "Artists later recalled how their fingers blistered and bled from constant work and how they slept under their desks rather than returning home."[49]

The Mighty Atom was so popular that in 1963 the cartoon was renamed *Astro Boy* and exported to the United States, where it was shown on Sunday mornings. (In 2009 the character was revived in the American computer-animated 3-D film *Astro Boy*.) With the success of *The Mighty Atom*, the press began referring to Tezuka by a new nickname, the "god of Anime."

The Mighty Atom generated a host of imitators. By 1965 three new anime studios opened in Tokyo and five new anime series appeared on Japanese TV. As the popularity of TV anime grew, the shows divided along the same gender lines that governed manga. Shōnen anime for boys featured battling warriors and monster robots. Shōjo anime for girls featured brave girls with magical superpowers, such as Princess Knight, who dressed like a boy when she fought evil.

The Walt Disney of the East

Tezuka was an influential role model to a generation of postwar Japanese artists who wished to pursue a career in anime. Hayao Miyazaki was one of those young animators. The popularity and influence of his hand-drawn artistic creations have led some to call him the Walt Disney of the East. And just as Disney's work in the 1930s is known as the golden era of Hollywood animation, the 1980s is known as the golden age of anime, largely because of Miyazaki.

Born in 1941, Miyazaki was drawn to anime after seeing the Toei production *The Tale of the White Serpent* (1958). Five years later Miyazaki was working as an animator at Toei, but his talents were seemingly overlooked for sixteen years. Although Miyazaki repeatedly tried to convince his bosses to allow him to write and direct an

Celebrating Astro Boy

When Osamu Tezuka created *The Mighty Atom*, or *Astro Boy*, in 1952, he wrote that the super-robot's birthday was on the far-distant date of April 7, 2003. In the years that followed, Tezuka turned *Astro Boy* into one of Japan's most iconic anime cartoon. The series, created with limited animation, was successful because Tezuka believe a good story can save poor animation, whereas good animation cannot save a bad story.

When Astro Boy's real birthday finally arrived on April 7, 2003, the Japanese held a national celebration. Eighty major corporations produced a massive array of *Astro Boy* toys, books, comics, and music that generated more than $5 billion. In addition, Tezuka, who died of stomach cancer at age sixty in 1989, was nationally acclaimed as *manga no kami*, the "god of anime." Today his work can be seen at the Osamu Tezuka Manga Museum, founded in 1994 in the small town of Takarazuka.

original anime, his requests were turned down. Miyazaki finally got to release his first effort, *The Castle of Cagliostro*, in 1979. Miyazaki not only cowrote and directed the story about a casino-robbing gentleman thief, he also acted as storyboardist and production designer. Despite the complicated story with dozens of settings, Miyazaki produced *The Castle of Cagliostro* in a little over five months. *The Castle of Cagliostro* was shown at the prestigious Cannes Film Festival, where it was praised by Steven Spielberg. This helped Miyazaki's next anime, *Nausicaä of the Valley of the Winds*, gain international attention.

Nausicaä of the Valley of the Winds follows Princess Nausicaä as she tries to avert war on a planet ravaged by toxic fungi, giant insects, and other environmental disasters. The characters in *Nausicaä* possess wide, expressive eyes and lipless mouths, much like the Mighty

Atom. However, Miyazaki's work was seen as unique by critics who praised him for creating characters and scenes that appeared realistic, even though they portrayed a bizarre fantasy world of the future. As critic Andrew Osmond writes, Miyazaki's work "has a commitment to cartoon naturalism. The technology and trappings may be outlandish, but the characters and details weave a coherent world. . . . Miyazaki's animation heightens rather than defines the various settings, with a weight on rich landscapes and well-observed detail. . . . *Nausicaa* resembles nothing so much as a detailed storyboard for a live-action film."[50]

With its rich landscapes and carefully crafted details *Nausicaä* was hailed as a masterpiece, and the success of the anime allowed Miyazaki to found Studio Ghibli in 1985 with longtime collaborator Isao Takahata. In the years that followed, Miyazaki produced numerous award-winning films, including *Kiki's Delivery Service* (1989) and *Princess Mononoke* (1997).

Stunning Hand-Drawn Images

Miyazaki's Oscar-winning *Spirited Away* (2001) was one of the highest-grossing films ever released in Japan, and it is estimated that one out of five Japanese people saw the anime. *Spirited Away* is a two-hour coming-of-age story mixed with fantasy and tinged with horror. The tale follows a sullen ten-year-old girl, Chihiro Ogino, as she encounters a magical world filled with a variety of unusual creatures. Created during the era of computer animation, *Spirited Away* is notable for its array of stunning images painted by hand, frame-by-frame, on cels. Movie critic Roger Ebert described *Spirited Away* as one of the best animated films ever made:

> Animation is a painstaking process, and there is a tendency to simplify its visual elements. Miyazaki, in contrast, offers complexity. His backgrounds are rich in detail, his canvas embraces space liberally, and it is all drawn with meticulous attention. We may not pay much conscious attention to the corners of the frame, but we know they are there, and they reinforce the remarkable precision of his fantasy worlds.[51]

Hayao Miyazaki, one of Japan's greatest animation artists, won an Academy Award for his 2001 film *Spirited Away*. Much of the film is set in a magical fantasy world filled with exquisite, hand-drawn landscapes and creatures.

In 2013, after releasing the historical fantasy anime *The Wind Rises*, the seventy-two-year-old Miyazaki announced his retirement. The anime production process is so slow, according to Miyazaki, that if he began another film, "it will take six or seven years to complete. . . . If I said I wanted to [make a feature film], I would sound like an old man saying something foolish."[52]

Akira's Influence

Although Miyazaki is retired, his work has influenced a generation of anime artists. When *The Castle of Cagliostro* was released, Katsuhiro Otomo was what the Japanese call an *otaku*, or obsessive anime and manga fan. In 1982 Otomo went from *otaku* to one of the most celebrated manga artists with the release of *Akira*. The six-volume manga series, which ran until 1990, filled a total of twenty-two-hundred pages. The epic was about psychotic teens with telekinetic powers creating havoc in Tokyo three decades after the city was destroyed in a nuclear holocaust.

Akira was so influential that Otomo was able to convince eight of Japan's largest media companies to produce an epic anime based on the story. The companies provided Otomo with $11 million to make *Akira*, a huge sum that made it the costliest anime of its time. Otomo shot *Akira* using 24 cels per second, which resulted in the creation 160,000 individual cels. He used a palette of 312 colors, which made *Akira* the richest hand-painted anime ever produced. This work resulted in detailed backgrounds and foregrounds, as well as exceptionally smooth motion. And when *Akira* was released in 1988, it became the number one Japanese box office success for the year. The following year, *Akira* was released in the United States and Europe, and the film is credited with starting an anime boom in the West.

> **Words in Context**
> *otaku*
> A Japanese nickname for people with an obsessive interest in manga and anime.

Americanime

Like numerous anime films imported to the United States in the late 1980s and early 1990s, *Akira* was filled with fast-moving violence, sexual activity, mutants, and cyborgs. With anime focused on subjects well beyond anything typically seen in American-made cartoons, the explicit Japanese style was appealing to older teens and those in their twenties. This fueled a demand for what is called *Americanime*, or Japanese anime dubbed in English; the Japanese soundtrack is removed and replaced with voices of American actors.

While *Akira* appealed to young men, a group of magical female crime fighters became one of the biggest anime sensations in American pop culture. The *Sailor Moon* series, created by manga artist Naoko Takeuchi, follows the blond superhero Sailor Moon and her Sailor Soldiers as they battle evil across the solar system. The two-hundred-episode anime series began running on the USA cable network in 1996 and moved to the Cartoon Network in 1998.

Despite its limited animation style of faded colors, blurry backgrounds, and barely moving facial features, *Sailor Moon* quickly caught on with American girls. Soon *Sailor Moon* was one of the most famous anime series in history, broadcast on nearly every continent. *Sailor Moon* spawned three feature films, several TV specials, a line of merchandise, video games, record albums, art books, and even a Broadway musical.

Sailor Moon sparked an interest in anime in the United States, and in 1997 the Cartoon Network began running a late-night block of action-oriented Americanime on a show called *Toonami*. In 2001 *Dragon Ball Z* became the fan favorite on *Toonami*. The show, created by

An anime artist in Japan creates digital images for an upcoming film. Some anime films feature hand-drawn characters and scenes while others rely on computer-generated imagery.

Spirited Away

Renowned film critic Roger Ebert considered Hayao Miyazaki's 2001 *Spirited Away* one of the best animated films ever made. *Spirited Away* follows ten-year-old Chihiro and her family on a drive after they get lost in a forest and end up at an abandoned amusement park where they find a cavernous floating bathhouse. Ebert describes the plot and artwork in *Spirited Away*:

> This is the beginning of an extraordinary adventure. Chihiro . . . will be placed under a spell by Yuba-ba, who steals her name and gives her a new one, Sen. Unless she can get her old name back again, she can never leave. One confusing space opens onto another in the bathhouse, whose population is a limitless variety of bizarre life-forms. There are little fuzzy black balls with two eyeballs, who steal Sen's shoes. Looming semi-transparent No Faces, who wear masks over their ghostly shrouds. Three extraordinary heads without bodies who hop about looking angry. . . . There is a malodorous heap of black slime, a river creature whose body has sopped up piles of pollution. Shape-shifting, so common in Japanese fantasy, takes place here, and the boy who first befriended her is revealed as a lithe sea dragon with fierce fangs.

Roger Ebert, "*Spirited Away*," RogerEbert.com, July 11, 2012. www.rogerebert.com.

Akira Toriyama, follows the exploits of a monkey-tailed alien raised by a kung fu master on earth. *Dragon Ball Z* consisted largely of long, pitched battles spread out over many episodes. This made it very popular with preteen boys. However, the show had an interesting animation style behind the kung fu fighters, according to reviewers

Brian Camp and Julie Davis: "[What is] noteworthy about *Dragon Ball* is the attention paid to the settings and landscapes. There are often beautiful nature scenes and backgrounds that resemble traditional charcoal paintings. The villages are often picturesque, representing a wide range of global settings."[53]

An International Phenomenon

Anime has dedicated fans in the United States, Europe, China, South Korea, and elsewhere. And the anime industry is a major component of Japan's economy. In 2013 there were more than 430 anime production studios in Japan producing thousands of animated movies a year. About 60 percent of those anime are based on successful manga. And they have influenced animators around the globe.

Anime features a cast of characters that includes spiky-haired teenage warriors, gun-wielding doe-eyed pixies, 50-foot (15 m) ninja warriors, and cuddly ogres. The blue and white robot cat Doraemon and the atomic Astro Boy are major celebrities in Japan and have become a part of world culture. By enticing fans to visit the world of the future or far distant planets where anything is possible, anime has become an international phenomenon that is moving faster than a rocket-powered robot.

Words in Context

dub

To replace the original language in a film with a different language; for example, when the dialogue in a Japanese anime is replaced with English.

Source Notes

Introduction: What Is the Art of Animation?

1. Vibeke Sorensen, "Philosophy Statement," University of Southern California, 2005. http://visualmusic.org.
2. John Canemaker, *Walt Disney's Nine Old Men and the Art of Animation*. New York: Disney Editions, 2001, p. 8.
3. Quoted in Esther Leslie, *Hollywood Flatlands: Animation, Critical Theory and the Avant-Garde*. New York: Verso, 2004, p. 286.
4. Marián Steiner, "Famous World Animators of the Past and the Present," *English and Film* (blog), April 3, 2013. http://english andfilm.wordpress.com.

Chapter One: Early Animation

5. Stefan Kanfer, *Serious Business*. New York: Scribner, 1997, pp. 22–23.
6. John Canemaker, *Windsor McCay: His Life and Art*. New York: Abrams, 2005, p. 97.
7. Quoted in Kanfer, *Serious Business*, p. 25.
8. Quoted in Danny Peary and Gerald Peary, eds., *The American Animated Cartoon*. New York: Dutton, 1980, p. 17.
9. Quoted in Canemaker, *Windsor McCay*, p. 163.
10. Canemaker, *Windsor McCay*, p. 160.
11. Quoted in Peary and Peary, *The American Animated Cartoon*, p. 24.
12. Charles Solomon, *Enchanted Drawings*. New York: Knopf, 1989, pp. 24–25.
13. Quoted in Peary and Peary, *The American Animated Cartoon*, p. 27.
14. Noell K. Wolfgram Evans, *Animators of Film and Television*. Jefferson, NC: McFarland, 2011, p. 54.
15. Quoted in Leslie Cabarga, *The Fleischer Story*. New York: Da Capo, 1988, p. 28.

16. Quoted in Gerald Carr, "Pat Sullivan," *Vixen*, 2013. www.vixen magazine.com.
17. Solomon, *Enchanted Drawings*, p. 33.
18. Quoted in Solomon, *Enchanted Drawings*, p. 34.

Chapter Two: Animation's Golden Age

19. Quoted in Michael Barrier, *Hollywood Cartoons*. New York: Oxford University Press, 1999, p. 50.
20. Quoted in Canemaker, *Walt Disney's Nine Old Men and the Art of Animation*, p. 14.
21. Canemaker, *Walt Disney's Nine Old Men and the Art of Animation*, p. 16.
22. Quoted in Barrier, *Hollywood Cartoons*, p. 116.
23. Michael Crandol, "The History of Animation: Advantages and Disadvantages of the Studio System in the Production of an Art Form," Digital Media FX, 1999. www.digitalmediafx.com.
24. Solomon, *Enchanted Drawings*, p. 59.
25. Solomon, *Enchanted Drawings*, p. 62.
26. Charles Solomon, "Fantastic Fantasia," *Los Angeles Times*, August 26, 1990. http://articles.latimes.com.

Chapter Three: Stop-Motion Animation

27. Quoted in Peter Lord and Brian Sibley, *Creating 3-D Animation*. New York: Abrams, 1998, p. 23.
28. Lord and Sibley, *Creating 3-D Animation*, p. 42.
29. Ray Harryhausen, "Pre-Dynamation," Official Ray Harryhausen Website, 2009. www.rayharryhausen.com.
30. Ray Harryhausen and Tony Dalton, *The Art of Ray Harryhausen*. New York: Billboard, 2006, p. 32.
31. Harryhausen and Dalton, *The Art of Ray Harryhausen*, p. 42.
32. Harryhausen and Dalton, *The Art of Ray Harryhausen*, p. 45.
33. Quoted in ComingSoon.net, "RIP Ray Harryhausen: 1920–2013," May 7, 2013. www.comingsoon.net.
34. Ian Drury, "Review: *The Adventures of Mark Twain*," *Seattle Examiner*, September 14, 2012. www.examiner.com.
35. Quoted in Owen Gibson, "A One-Off Quirky Thing," *Guardian* (London), July 20, 2008. www.theguardian.com.
36. Quoted in Laura Frances, "Interview: Tim Burton on 'Frankenweenie,' Stop-Motion and Old Monster Films," ScreenCrave, October 4, 2012. http://screencrave.com.

Chapter Four: Computer-Generated Animation

37. Quoted in Lisa Fitzpatrick, *The Art of Avatar*. New York: Abrams, 2009, p. 15.
38. Fitzpatrick, *The Art of Avatar*, p. 15.
39. Quoted in Fitzpatrick, *The Art of Avatar*, p. 7.
40. Kevin Holmes, "Original Creators: Visionary Computer Animator John Whitney Sr.," *The Creators Project* (blog), June 11, 2012. http://thecreatorsproject.vice.com.
41. John Whitney Sr., "Notes on *Permutations*," Center for Visual Music, 2012. www.centerforvisualmusic.org.
42. Quoted in Bonnie Miller, "The John Whitney Biography Page," SIGGRAPH, 2010. www.siggraph.org.
43. Quoted in Maureen Furniss, *Art in Motion: Animation Aesthetics*. Eastleigh, UK: Libbey, 2007, p. 188.
44. Brian Sibley, *The Lord of the Rings: The Making of the Movie Trilogy*. New York: Houghton Mifflin, 2002, p. 166.
45. Quoted in Anne Thompson, "How James Cameron's Innovative New 3D Tech Created *Avatar*," *Popular Mechanics*, January 2, 2010. www.popularmechanics.com.

Chapter Five: Anime

46. Quoted in Roger Ebert, "*Spirited Away*," RogerEbert.com, July 11, 2012. www.rogerebert.com.
47. Quoted in Natsu Onoda Power, *God of Comics: Osamu Tezuka and the Creation of Post–World War II Manga*. Jackson: University Press of Mississippi, 2009, p. 42.
48. Quoted in Mark W. MacWilliams, *Japanese Visual Culture: Explorations in the World of Manga and Anime*. Armonk, NY: Sharpe, 2008, p. 124.
49. Simon Richmond, *The Rough Guide to Anime*. London: Rough Guides, 2009, p. 12.
50. Andrew Osmond, "Nausicaa and the Fantasy of Hayao Miyazaki," *Foundation*, Spring 1998. www.nausicaa.net.
51. Ebert, "*Spirited Away*."
52. Quoted in Brian Ashcraft, "Hayao Miyazaki Explains Why He's Retiring," *Kotaku* (blog), September 6, 2013. http://kotaku.com.
53. Brian Camp and Julie Davis, *Anime Classics Zettai!* Berkeley, CA: Stone Bridge, 2012, p. 110.

For Further Research

Books

Kathy Furgang, *Careers in Digital Animation*. New York: Rosen, 2013.

J.B. Kaufman, *Snow White and the Seven Dwarfs: The Art and Creation of Walt Disney's Classic Animated Film*. San Francisco: Walt Disney Family Foundation, 2012.

Jeff Lenburg, *Hayao Miyazaki*. New York: Facts On File, 2012.

Jeff Lenburg, *John Lasseter: The Whiz Who Made Pixar King*. New York: Chelsea House, 2012.

Helen McCarthy and Katsuhiro Otomo, *The Art of Osamu Tezuka: God of Manga*. Lewes, UK: Ilex, 2013.

Hayao Miyazaki, *Art of Princess Mononoke*. San Francisco: VIZ Media, 2014.

Charles Solomon, *The Toy Story Films: An Animated Journey*. New York: Disney Editions, 2012.

Walt Disney Animation Research Library, *Animation*. New York: Disney Editions, 2009.

Websites

Aardman Animations (www.aardman.com). This site is home to the British animation studio that produced numerous animated and stop-motion movies, TV shows, and commercials, including *The Pirates! In an Adventure with Scientists!* and *Wallace and Gromit: The Curse of the Were-Rabbit*. The site features many photos and drawings, with links to company history, productions, and podcasts. The "Studio Tour" page takes visitors through the numerous steps necessary to create an animation, including storyboarding, model making, and filming.

Animation World Network (www.awn.com). The latest news about animation and anime, with interviews, blogs, trailers, and events. The "Anime" section features the latest theatrical and DVD releases.

Anime News Network (www.animenewsnetwork.com). A comprehensive site covering anime, with news, clips of latest releases, discussion forums, and an encyclopedia of terms and titles.

Bray Animation Project (http://brayanimation.weebly.com). This site is dedicated to John R. Bray, one of the earliest mass producers of animated cartoons. Visitors can learn about the history of Bray Productions, the films produced by the animation company, and the artistic details of cartoons enjoyed by millions during the 1910s and 1920s.

50 Greatest Cartoons (http://tvtropes.org/pmwiki/pmwiki.php /Main/The50GreatestCartoons). In 1994 animation historian Jerry Beck polled one thousand animators and historians to compile a list of the fifty all-time best cartoons. This site lists each cartoon, the lead animator, the year it was created, and often-comical analyses of plots and animation.

Newgrounds (www.newgrounds.com). This entertainment and social media site founded in 1995 hosts hundreds of user-generated Adobe Flash animations, games, music videos, and art. Visitors can choose projects from various categories, including latest, greatest, and most popular. The "Team Up!" section provides a forum for writers, artists, musicians, voice actors, and programmers to find like-minded collaborators.

Official Ray Harryhausen Website (www.rayharryhausen.com). A site featuring the words and work of stop-motion animation superstar Ray Harryhausen. It is run by the foundation Harryhausen founded with his wife, Diana, to archive, preserve, and restore his extensive collections for exhibit, educational, and enjoyment purposes.

Pixar (www.pixar.com). This website, hosted by one of the world's premier animation studios, features an inside look at Pixar's feature films, from *Toy Story* to *Monsters University*, along with short films and behind-the-scenes videos featuring directors, character designers, animators, and others.

Tezuka in English (http://tezukainenglish.com). A site dedicated to the Japanese artist who drew more than 150,000 pages of manga in his forty-year career and launched the TV anime revolution with the creation of *Astro Boy*.

Vimeo (http://vimeo.com/categories/animation). This popular video-sharing website attracts 65 million unique visitors every month. The "Animation & Motion Graphics" page is divided into several categories, including 2-D, 3-D, computer animation, flash, and stop-motion. The community (called Vimeans) includes dozens of indie filmmakers and their fans.

Index

Picture Credits

Cover: Thinkstock Images

Maury Aaseng: 40

© AP/Corbis: 14

Photofest New York: 5, 11, 16, 21, 31, 48, 50, 54, 66

© Lefteris Pitarakis/AP/Corbis: 36

© Louie Psihoyos/Corbis: 27

© Louis Quail/In Pictures/Corbis: 43

Thinkstock Images: 61

© TWPhoto/Corbis: 68